Comments on the Book of

Jeremiah

WITH RELECTIONS AND EXPLANATIONS
REGARDING THE DEEPER CHRISTIAN LIFE

by
Jeanne Guyon

Jeremiah
All *new* material in this edition
copyrighted by SeedSowers Publishing House
Printed in the United States of America
All rights reserved

Published by The SeedSowers
              P.O. Box 3317
              Jacksonville, FL 32206
              1-800-228-2665
              www.seedsowers.com

Library of Congress Cataloging - in - Data
              Guyon, Jeanne
              Jeremiah / Jeanne Guyon
              ISBN 0-940232-92-8
              1. Commentary

Times New Roman 13 pt.

Books by Jeanne Guyon

Experiencing the Depths of Jesus Christ
Final Steps in Christian Maturity
Intimacy with Christ
Spiritual Torrents
Union with God
Autobiography of Jeanne Guyon

Commentaries by Jeanne Guyon

Genesis
Exodus
Leviticus - Numbers - Deuteronomy
Judges
Job
Song of Songs
Jeremiah
James - First John - Revelation

also

The Life of Jeanne Guyon *(T.C. Upham)*

Publisher's Note:

In this volume Jeanne Guyon did not comment on every verse and chapter. Rather, she selected certain verses. You will also find some passages archaic in language and in spelling.

Introduction

Jeremiah was a prophet, a native of Anathoth, a priestly city in the tribe of Benjamin; and was sanctified from his mother's womb, to be a prophet of God: which office he began to execute when he was yet a child in age. He was in his whole life, according to the signification of his name, great before the Lord; and a special figure of Jesus Christ, in the persecutions he underwent for discharging his duty; in his charity for his persecutors; and in the violent death he suffered at their hands; it being an ancient tradition of the Hebrews, that he was stoned to death by the remnant of the Jews who had retired into Egypt when the Chaldean Governor Godoliah, had been murdered.

Who collected the scrolls Jeremiah gave forth cannot, perhaps, be known with certainty, but Baruch, who has been called a prophet, is said to have been his amanuensis.

The Prophecy of Jeremiah

CHAPTER I.

Jer. 1:4   *Before I formed you in the bowels of your mother I knew you: and before you came forth out of the womb I sanctified you, and made you a prophet unto the nations.*

That which is here stated of Jeremiah, may also be understood as referring to every soul that is called by God to his special service. He has chosen them from the *beginning*, even before they came forth into life; in their *very origin* He has specially consecrated them, and given them their mission among the children of men. And God makes these souls go forth to the outer world according to His eternal designs, and establishes them as prophets among the nations. But these special calls are very *rare* indeed.

Jer. 1:6   *And I said: Ah, ah, ah Lord God: Behold I cannot speak for I am a child.*

Those whom God sends forth to assist others,

generally consider themselves unfit, not having the least inclination for this service, but longing to dwell hidden and unknown. This threefold ah, ah, ah! and the expressive objection, show the astonishment of the prophet who can find in himself nothing but entire incapacity. He considers himself powerless on account of the lack of natural talents and also, because he possesses no inclination to stand forth as a special servant. He sees himself unworthy in the sight of God to carry his message of the Eternal Word; and furthermore, he finds that he is but a child and too young, being only just brought forth in the regeneration of God himself. But though he alleges this as a disqualification it is the best qualification for his mission: for he must become entirely childlike that he may not mix the speech of man with the language that God gives.

Jer. 1:7-9   The Lord said to me—say not I am a child; for you shall go to all that I shall send you; and whatsoever I command you shall speak. Be not afraid at their presence; for I am with you to deliver you, says the Lord. Then the Lord put forth His hand and touched my mouth, and the Lord said to me: Behold, I have put my words in your mouth.

Jeremiah had all the qualities of a truly great missionary. He was simple and nothing but a child, incapable of mixing that which is human with that which is divine; he was entirely given over to God, in a frame of mind to go wherever he was sent by the Lord, because he was not attached to any place or object, he had no possessions of his own, nor any certain form of speech; therefore God said unto him: "Whatsoever I shall command you shall speak, and nothing else. I myself will put my words into your mouth; for through my Almighty power, which is as it were a touch of the hand, I make you one with myself in closest union." After this *central* touch, and this essential *union* being the mouth of the soul (for self-will has there no more influence), the Word is brought forth in the soul; wherefore God says: "I have put my speech, which is my Word, in your mouth, even the Word in the very center of your soul; this is my true speech, and you shall utter none but this, which shall be your word and mine. You shall be nothing but a channel, a pure vessel to carry my word, wherever it desires to be taken to. Even this word which you shall carry will bear itself, and I will act similarly with you.

> *Jer. 1:10*   *Lo I have set you this day over the nations, and over kingdoms, to root up, and to pull down, and to build, and to plant.*

O Lord, my God, what words are these! You send forth your prophet to pluck up, and to break down, to destroy and to overthrow, O Lord, as great a prophet as this is required; yea, even as consecrated as was John the Baptist (Matt. 3:3), to prepare your ways in the soul. You are not able to hold your entrance in her, until everything which is not yourself— however sublime it may appear to be—be plucked up, destroyed and lost, without keeping back anything: for if there remain *an atom of self*, you can not come in. But, you destroy and pull down, that you might build up and plant. Even to plant there Jesus the Christ, in intimate oneness for ever and ever, that *He* may be born within, and proclaimed without; O Jeremiah, you are truly the prophet who prepares souls for the coming of the Messiah! Isaiah foretold His coming, and you go still further, traveling like John the Baptist to prepare His *Way.*

> *Jer. 1:11, 12   And the Word of the Lord came to me saying: What do you see, Jeremiah? And I said: I see a rod watching. And the Lord said to me: You have seen well: for I will watch over My Word to perform it.*

The Word of the Lord has been brought forth in this soul, as says the Apostle Paul: "I am again in travail until the Christ be formed in you" (Gal. 4:19), and then she understands a *great* truth, which is as the early blossoming rod of the almond tree, ever *watching* to bloom forth. This rod signifies the ruling power of God, and the fitness of His Word, which is ever ready to blossom forth in the soul, if the soul is but ready to make room for it. This *straight* rod keeps watching over the soul to protect her, and also *watches* like the early blossoming almond branch to blossom forth as the Word in the soul, whenever she is prepared for it, and to show *visible* fruit whenever required according to the will of God. The soul on her part is also always turning *straight* towards her God in an admirable attitude, never quitting this *straightforward* rectitude towards her God and this *watchfulness* for Him. God Himself incessantly watches over His

Word, for *He* is always the same, and by the outpouring of Himself, bringing forth this Word, producing the same without even creating it; but for the *outer world*, and for the *creature*, God speaks and brings it to pass.

CHAPTER II.

Jer. 2:1   And the Word of the Lord was brought forth in me..

This is to say, Christ came forth within me as the creative Word—the Word-God, to enable me to go into all the world and proclaim and preach him.

Jer. 2:2   I have remembered you, pitying your youth, and the love of your espousals, when you followed Me in the desert, in a land that is not sown.

God pitied the soul in the state of probation He made her pass through: and the greater the trial, the stronger is the compassion God has for her.

Jer. 2:12, 13   Be astonished, O you heavens at this, and you gates thereof be very desolate, says the Lord. For My people have done two evils. They have forsaken Me, the fountain of living water, and have dug to themselves cisterns, broken cisterns, that can hold no water.

O you souls, already quite celestial, and you who wander in the path of self-denial, which is like the gate that leads to God, be in astonishment and sadness, for behold the people of God, which He has chosen for Himself, to whom He would give (John 4:14; 7:38) streams of living water flowing from Himself and springing up in them to everlasting life, have left this source of living water to enjoy themselves in their own creaturely activity by digging wells with holes in them, that cannot retain the water. Here we should remember that the fountains, and sources, are the works of God Himself, but the cisterns are altogether of the creature. God is grieved that man, who might have the water of life so easily by merely committing himself into God's keeping, goes nevertheless about all his life long amusing himself in digging cisterns, yes with infinite pain, without any real use, for these cisterns dug by the hand of man are altogether full of defects, and cannot keep the water of life.

> *Jer. 2:22   Though you wash yourself with nitre (lye), and multiply to yourself the herb borith (an herb used for cleansing), you are stained in your iniquity before Me, says the Lord.*

O God, there is no one who can cleanse us from our secret faults, which is all we have in our innermost parts, but You and You alone; however much we try to cleanse ourselves in our own strength, however clean we may appear in our own eyes, we can but always remain polluted and impure in Your holy sight, until You Yourself have purified us in our inward parts from that impurity which possesses our very soul.

> *Jer. 2:23   How can you say: I am not pol-*
> *luted. I have not walked after Baalim? See your*
> *ways in the valley, know what you have done: as*
> *a swift runner pursuing his course.*

How can the souls, which God has not cleansed from their inherent pollution, say that they are not impure? In humiliation of soul they will have to learn and discern what they have committed in their earthly pilgrimage. Then they will acknowledge that whatsoever appeared pure unto them was nothing but the greatest impurity.

CHAPTER III.

Jer. 3:14   *Return, O you revolting children, says the Lord, for I am your husband, and I will take you, one of a city, and two of a kindred, and will bring you into Zion.*

God invites us all to return to Him with the same confidence as the wife returns to her husband. I will receive you, and take you to Myself, says the Lord, as soon as you will return to Me. You may return to Me and prepare yourself to commune with Me just like the wife desires to be one with her husband. To this oneness we are all called, but alas! We find no one who can help us to make this turning to the Lord a reality, or who can lead us to the *oneness with God.* God will take us Himself, and bring us to our center. Nevertheless, we will not give Him our hand; but address ourselves to the creatures, who turn away from us.

Jer 3:15   *And I will give you shepherds according to My own heart, and they shall feed you with knowledge and understanding.*

11

God sees that almost every disorder and misery arises because there are no shepherds who conduct souls straight to Him. He, therefore, promises to those who will really return to Him with their whole heart that He will send them shepherds according to His own heart, who will lead them in the straight way, and who will feed them with the true wisdom and the understanding of truth, guiding the souls to give to God what they owe to Him, and leaning upon no one but Himself.

> Jer. 3:20-22 *But as a woman that despises her lover, so has the house of Israel despised Me, says the Lord. A voice was heard in the highways, weeping and howling of the children of Israel: because they have made their way wicked, they have forgotten the Lord their God. Return, you rebellious children, and I will heal your rebellions. Behold, we come to You: for You are the Lord, our God.*

Ah, what a deplorable case! God, with infinite goodness, calls upon the soul to return to Him; but this ungrateful soul despises her Lord, by whom she is loved. O Love, who finds it not beneath Yourself to declare Yourself to be her Lover; and yet the soul is so unkind that she despises Him to whom she owes everything. But Your tender care leaves her not to herself on account of her repeated ingratitude; for though this soul, which You call to Yourself, and for which You are waiting to give Yourself to her, forgets You: You unchangeably call her to Yourself with words full of tender care: Oh, you, My children, for whom I yearn with the heart of a Father, be converted to Me; even after you have turned away from Me, turn again to Me; and I Myself will heal all the evil you have done. God asks nothing more than to return to Him, even as we have turned away from Him, and He will bring about all the rest. Thus the people of Israel, having left the guidance of God, did nothing else than turn again to God; and as soon as they returned wholly and sincerely, God showed the same kindness to them and was their *Guide*. Therefore, the people respond to God saying: Behold, we come again to You, for You are the Lord our God, guide us according to Your will.

> Jer 3:23 *In very deed the hills were liars, and the multitude of the mountains: truly in the Lord our God is the salvation of Israel.*

When the soul has been enlightened through her return to God, understanding that whatsoever appears most grand and most elevated in the guidance of man, is nothing but lies and failure, and that the true life of the soul, given entirely to God, must be *in* God, she may well exclaim: "Oh, what a happy state, to have turned to the Lord, to be absorbed in Him; He guides the soul into Himself, where she finds eternal life."

Chapter IV.

Jer. 4:1   *If you will return, O Israel, says the Lord, return to Me, if you will take away your stumbling blocks out of My sight, you shall not be moved.*

O Lord, if all Your state of bliss *depended* on the return of this soul, You could not persuade her more forcibly and with greater tenderness. You are the supplicant, You promise and entreat in a thousand ways, saying You ask nothing else than this sincere return, and they will not believe You! O Israel, if you will return to Me, says this God of compassion, how happy I will make you. O you souls, whom I have chosen for Myself, I am waiting for nothing more than your return; in tender mercy I ask it of you: and you refuse to listen! Be converted to Me, and merely put away these stumbling blocks to our oneness and I will unite Myself with you. How admirable is this expression: Take away your stumbling blocks out of My sight. The hindrance to our seeing God's face consists in our having turned away from Him; in this state we cannot have the sweet smile of His countenance influencing us. But no sooner has the soul turned towards God, than His countenance beams upon her, and every obstacle that prevented His divine influence has been taken away. O soul! If you will but remove this single obstacle to My union with you, I will little by little draw you to Me and when you have been united to Me, you need not be anxious about anything, for no harm can befall that soul whose Protector I am.

> *Jer. 4:2*   *And you shall swear: As the Lord lives, in truth, and in judgment and in justice: and the Gentiles shall bless Him and shall praise Him.*

Then you will no longer trust to yourself, but you will assure everyone that the Master lives in you and that you are living in Him: that in truth He lives there so as to show forth His truth, that He exercises judgment and spreads His righteousness there: that *out of* this oneness there is *nothing* but *death, falsehood, folly* and *unrighteousness.* God puts His understanding into the mind: His righteousness into the memory: His truth into the heart and will, or, we may say better still: He puts there three things at the same time into our capacities, filling heart and spirit with *righteousness, judgment* and *truth.* Then the Lord is praised and blessed among the nations who were invited to enter on this way, and procure for themselves so great a blessing: all who taste and experience this are overflowing with transports of joy.

> *Jer 4:4*   *Be circumcised to the Lord and take away the foreskins of your hearts, you men of Judah.*

To be circumcised unto God is to be made *free* and *separated* from everything that is not of God. The soul that turns to her Lord becomes at the same time removed from that which is in contradiction with Him: whereas she who approaches anything contrary to God necessarily moves away from Him. What is this circumcision of the heart? It is the cutting away of all self-will that belongs to the heart; and this is done by abandoning ourselves entirely to God's will. Behold this is the conversion in which consists the whole travail of the soul.

> *Jer. 4:23-25*   *I beheld the earth, and lo, it was void and nothing: and the heavens, and there was no light in them. I looked upon the mountains: and behold they trembled, and all the hills were troubled. I beheld, and lo, there was no man: and all the birds of the air were gone.*

See here the description of the soul in the state of *nothingness*. Of that which is her own she has become entirely *void* and *empty*: there is nothing in the world remaining her own, however insignificant it may appear: yes, heaven has become obscured to her, for there exists no connection between the superior and the inferior, they are quite separated.

Then the souls, in a higher phase of experience, fear and tremble for such a soul. If she could see herself in this state, she would be in terrible apprehension, and when God permits her to see herself, her very being is shaken by fear, and her faculties are filled with alarm: the *spirit* is then quite obscured, without any light, and nothing of man remains, for every reliance has been taken away, and the facility with which the soul hastened to that which is good has gone. Man in this state has no knowledge remaining in him, every light has given way to the will of God. The birds of heaven, those souls raised into light in the blissful state already, have withdrawn from them: for if that state should be spoken of, they could not comprehend it, because they are far from desiring to embrace it.

> *Jer 4:26   I looked, and behold Carmel was a wilderness: and all its cities were destroyed at the presence of the Lord.*

When God Himself wishes to take possession of the soul, everything else must give place to *Him*: that is why everything else is destroyed and there appears nothing but a wilderness.

CHAPTER V.

Jer 5:3   *O Lord, Your eyes are upon truth.*

God has regard for nothing else in the soul but truth, faith in Him. This faith in God brings it about that He does not look upon our manifold defects, but Jesus said, I will, be made clean: and according to our faith in Him who is "the Truth," will it be done to us.

CHAPTER VII.

Jer. 7:28   *This is the nation which has not listened to the voice of their God, nor received instruction.*

There is no longer any faith—truth—among them. The proof of our faith may be seen in our listening to the voice of God in us, and in the accepting cheerfully every cross, worry, and affliction, that comes upon us from time to time. But those who will not listen to their God, nor suffer for His cause, will lose little by little whatever of faith and truth there may have been in them.

CHAPTER IX.

Jer. 9:23-24   *Let not the wise man glory in his wisdom, and let not the strong man glory in his strength, and let not the rich man glory in his riches. But let him that glories glory in this, that he understands and knows Me, for I am the Lord that exercises mercy, and judgment, and justice in the earth: for these things please me, says the Lord.*

God does not want the wise man to glory in his wisdom, nor in his strength, nor in his gifts or his graces, which are has riches, for all these perish: but let him glory in God, that he knows all his wisdom, strength and riches are in the Lord, that in himself man is nothing but weakness, folly and poverty, that it is God's work to operate in the soul through His grace, to fulfill all righteousness in her, for God alone is all in all. This wisdom is pleasing to God; but not the knowledge of the wise in their own eyes, or the strength of the strong, for God can soon take away all these things.

CHAPTER X.

Jer. 10:21   Because the pastors have done foolishly and have not sought the Lord: therefore they have not understood, and all their flock is scattered.

Almost every defect in the advancement of souls is due to their teachers: for these do not seek the Lord with all their heart, nor do they listen to Him, that they may understand His guidance: they do not teach these things to their flocks: therefore the sheep are scattered and remain in the dispersion and in error without returning to God.

Jer. 10:23-24   I know, O Lord, that the way of a man is not his: neither is it in a man to walk, and to direct his steps. Correct me, O Lord, but yet with judgment: and not in Thy fury.

Though the way of a man may not be of his own choosing, he may always choose to give himself wholly to God: and we ought to do this the more readily as we know our inability to walk in our own strength. God is always ready to lead and to enable the soul to walk, who gives herself entirely to Him. The prophet therefore asks to be corrected by the judgment of God, for this correction enables the soul to return to God: he desires nothing but his justice, for the judgment of God is mercy altogether. This is the inheritance of the souls who walk in the way of the cross and in faith and not in God's fury, which belongs to the wicked. God chastises whomsoever He loves with mercy: but wickedness will be punished by His wrath.

Chapter XI.

*Jer. 11:3   Cursed is the man who will not lis-
ten to the words of the covenant.*

The Lord speaks to man in no other than words of
peace and of unity, and happy is he who listens to God
speaking in him: but he who will not listen cannot be
happy, and never possesses true peace, for he is not in
unity with the God of peace.

*Jer. 11:4   Hear My voice and do all things
that I command you: and you shall be My people,
and I will be your God.*

God recommends to us nothing else than to
listen to His voice and to obey Him by following no
other will than *His*. He who listens to the Lord and
does *His* will, belongs to God in a special manner,
and God belongs to him.

CHAPTER XII.

Jer. 12:11   With desolation is all the land made desolate: because there is none that consider in the heart.

To think or to speak in the heart means to be in unity with the will of God. That in the heart is the true presence of God, and those who have this presence in the heart, are in the beginning of perfection: and all the barrenness and desolation that arises in the soul comes from our forgetfulness of God. Nothing is easier than to obtain this presence of God in the heart: by seeking Him with a faithful consideration of our hearts. By keeping close to Him in a disposition of humble waiting: our soul soon shall discover her God, who will show Himself to her in such manner that it can be experienced better than explained.

CHAPTER XIII.

Jer. 13:1, 3, 4   Thus says the Lord to me: Go, and get a linen girdle, and put it about your loins, and do not put it into water. And the word of the Lord came to me the second time saying: Take the girdle which you got, which is about your loins, and arise, go to the Euphrates, and hide it there in a hole of the rock.

God desires that the soul shall divest herself of all that self-righteousness which she made for herself, and be adorned in the *true* righteousness which is altogether *God's* own. And when she is put into the vesture God has chosen, when she is again His by right of creation, then He does not permit her to bathe again, as it were, in that stream, or to wash her garment in the polluted waters, which she had stooped to before. Such washing would indicate her abasement and a mixing again with the fleeting perishing things of the world. On the contrary, the soul has to hide her righteousness in the secret of *"the rock,"* that she may be preserved there and kept safe against all pride. But man, nevertheless, wants to oppose all this: he hides his own righteousness in *himself*, trusting he may preserve it there, and ultimately appear as the rightful owner of it.

> *Jer. 13:6, 7, 9   After many days the Lord said to me: Arise, go to the Euphrates, and take from there the girdle which I commanded you to hide there. And behold the girdle was rotten so that it was fit for no use. Thus said the Lord: After this manner will I make the pride of Judah, and the great pride of Jerusalem to rot.*

Oh, Lord God, how wonderful are the figures which it pleased You to set forth in the Holy Scriptures of the things belonging to the interior life of the soul! The Most High condescends to the doing of such small matters as appear to the human judgment quite unworthy of God's dignity. At the same time the Lord brings about through these insignificant affairs two great results, the one is to show forth admirable mysteries under figures that appear low, the other that He may thus exercise the faith and obedience of those whom He gets to do these small things. Our worldly-wise and so-called strong minds treat these facts as illusions and trifling aberrations. Still, the Lord has decided otherwise. These things God considered not unworthy of His attention, and has given them a place in the Holy Scriptures. This *hidden girdle*, now shows the self-righteousness stowed away by the owner, who has become excellent in his own eyes, and is filled with vain glory: approving of his own deeds, and feeling safe on account of the great esteem which he knows full well he is carrying about in his own bosom. But, behold what happens to all this self-righteousness? When the owner least expects it, the whole stock of it becomes rotten, destroys itself. There is no cohesion in this girdle, it does not please God, it is profitable to no one, not even to the owner: it calls by its very putrescence for the means of purification, that the soul may become enlightened.

> *Jer. 13:11   As the girdle sticks close to the loins of a man, so have I brought close to Me all the house of Israel, and all the house of Judah, says the Lord: that they might be My people: and for a name, and for a praise, and for a glory: but they would not hear.*

Oh, Lord God, with whom are You desirous of uniting Yourself so closely? With Your people, even those abandoned to You. Yes, You have *done* it; You *have* intimately united Yourself with them. And when we leave ourselves to be so entirely given over to God, then we are the very name, the glory, and the praise of the Lord. For there is nothing in those truly abandoned to God that is not *with* God, and *for* God. Every talent which they may possess, whatsoever their station in life may be, their existence or nonexistence, their self-surrender and abandonment, all and everything, is changed into the glory and praise of the Most High. But oh, how many disunite themselves from so good a Heavenly Father, how they live without God! They will not listen to THE WORD in them, by which God called them back to Himself that they might become partakers of the *new* and Heavenly Life.

> *Jer. 13:16   Give glory to the Lord your God,*

before it is dark, and before your feet stumble upon the dark mountains: when you shall look for light, and He will turn it into the shadow of death, and into obscurity.

We must glorify the Lord before it be too late, before the soul may be put into darkness, into the obscurity of death, for then she can do nothing. And how is God to be glorified in us? We glorify the Lord by abandoning ourselves to all His requirements, to His *entire* will. For the soul who gives herself not *altogether* up to God, deceives herself, in that she always looks for some new illustrations or greater illuminations: she is mistaken in this one essential point of entire abandonment, she will not find the revelations she longs for. Yes, God has put the true life into the shadow of *the mystic death.* It may appear paradoxical, that we are to find *light* in deep *darkness*, and meet with darkness in the very light: that *death* may be found in *life,* and *true life* in the *mystic death.*

> *Jer. 13:18   Say to the king, and to the queen: humble yourselves, sit down: for the crown of your glory is come down from your head.*

The mind of man is the king, and the will is the queen. Both have to bow down and humble themselves, and become nothing, and be very low in their own nothingness: for the glory of their beautiful crown has been taken away from them. Reason is the crown of the spirit, and the glory thereof. God takes away, and forbids every use of this noble faculty. To will good actions, and to desire their accomplishment is the glory of the human will: God dethrones and destroys every creaturely desire.

CHAPTER XV.

Jer. 15:16   Your words were found, and I ate them: and Your words were to me a joy and the rejoicing of my heart.

As soon as the soul discovers THE WORD of God in herself, she partakes of the same as of some precious food, delighting greatly in the abundance. The heart is filled with rejoicing: and the joyous life of the soul is sustained on the glory of the Living Word. Oh, the blissful solitude of that soul in which God is heard! It is not a loud, beautiful, distinct tone. It is a *"still small voice,"* the very *muteness* of which, is so *plaintive* that only the soul entirely given over to God, can distinguish the sound of the Word breathing in her.

The will of God filling the soul makes the Word heard: yes, God's will in *her* breaks the Word as bread and thus nourishes her with Life everlasting. Those who have experienced these things will find the above passage of Scripture very suggestive and beautiful.

Jer. 15:17   I did not sit in the assembly of jesters, nor did I make a boast of the presence of Your hand: I sat alone because You have filled me with threats.

The prophet did not set forth what *he* has done, as if *he* deserved any praise: he glories in the strength of the Almighty, by whose power *alone* he was what he was. The divine power (declares the prophet), works in me for the glory of God, in which I have no part. He, himself, sat alone and remained separated from every creaturely activity, whether the same came from others or belonged to himself, he sat in *lowliness* indeed, being nothing at all in himself, entirely revealing to the divine Light his own unworthiness within and without.

> *Jer. 15:18   Why is my pain perpetual, and my wound incurable, which refused to heal?*

When the time of anguish is upon the soul, in which it pleased God to lead her and reduce her into a dying state, into the days of her very death: then her pain appears as of perpetual duration, she can see no end to it, despair is upon her. There is then a wound in the soul (as it were), which stands open and will not close: incurable, refusing to be healed. And the pain becomes natural to the soul: and because the wound is such an ancient one, it seems to become agreeable: yes the soul apprehends that she herself may be refusing to be healed.

> *Jer. 15:19   Therefore, the Lord says: If you return, then I will bring you back again, that you may stand before Me: and if you take forth the precious from the vile, you shall be as My mouth.*

It is not God who is regardless of us, nor is His grace ever exhausted. No sooner does the soul desire to return to Him from whom she has gone so far away, then the Lord says: "I will bring you back again." We know, too well, that the soul cannot in her own strength perform this "returning," and therefore, she needs to leave herself in His care and keeping: God will do it. And in God's own strength He will enable her to stand before Him in *His very presence.* Oh, how God will qualify the soul, how He will in His love enable her to sound forth His praises! But to this end, it is necessary that she should distinguish and separate what is of God, which is *precious,* from that which is of man, and is *vile.* Yes, then, she shall be as God's mouth, to make known *His* glory among the children of men. This taking forth "the precious from the vile" puts the soul in a condition to attribute to God all that is good, and herself all that is evil: it enables her to see, that in so much as God cannot be the author of evil, man can *in his own strength* bring forth no good of any kind.

CHAPTER XVII.

Jer. 17:5   Cursed is the man that trusts in man, and makes flesh his arm, and whose heart departs from the Lord.

Almost all men are quite willing to trust in some other men, but no one is (naturally) willing to trust *solely* in his God. Blessed is he who leans upon nothing else but his God. But misery overcomes him who relies on that which belongs to the creature: yes, *lost* is the man, who finds his strength in the arm of flesh, and not in the all-sufficient power of God. Such a man, departs from God, even though he desires to get near *Him*.

Jer 17:7   Blessed is the man that trusts in the Lord and whose hope the Lord is.

Oh, Lord God, You Yourself have said, that he who trusts solely in You is blessed: He is in a safe place; hidden, so that no real evil can find him; he shall not perish. Though a time may come to him, when evil surrounds him; every misfortune shall make him surer of the life. But the apparent prosperity of those who confide in that which is human brings them death.

> *Jer. 17:13   O Lord, the hope of Israel! All that forsake You shall be written in the earth, because they have forsaken the Lord, the fountain of living waters.*

You truly, O Lord, are the rest and hope of the souls who *abandon* themselves to You! Whoever leaves You shall be ashamed! All who confide in themselves, and their own devices, in things earthly—will be written and even buried among those very earthly things. But the souls who abandon themselves to You, are written in *Your* bosom. They who depart from You, have left the fountain of living waters to drink of the turbid streams of earth: they shall have their fill.

> *Jer. 17:14   Heal me, O Lord, and I shall be healed, save me, and I shall be saved: for You are my praise—my glory.*

O Lord God! You alone can save me! I desire no other health than that which You give me: My salvation is in Your hands! If *You* save me, then I shall be saved *indeed*: and I desire no other salvation than Yours. You are my glory and my praise. I am satisfied and content that You are such as You are. I do not desire that anything of mine should praise You, but that You should be praised by Your own glory.

CHAPTER XVIII.

*Jer. 18:3-6   I went down to the potter's house.
And when the vessel that he made of the clay was
marred in the hand of the potter, he made it again
another vessel, as seemed good to the potter to
make it. Then the word of the Lord came to me
saying, O house of Israel, cannot I do with you as
this potter? Says the Lord, Behold, as the clay in
the potter's hand, so are you in My hand, O house
of Israel.*

God gives us in these passages of Scripture a
very striking insight into the power that He has over
the soul, and how it is nothing but right that she should
abandon herself to Him. Oh, Lord God, how true
this is! Are You not all-powerful to destroy and to
build again? Oh, may it please You to work in us and
through us, as You know best? When *most lost* and
destroyed we are *most safe*: when we imaging ourselves to be most safe, then we are most lost. Let us
be passive and without any resistance in God's hands,
even as a vessel in the hands of the potter: let God
turn us as He pleases. He can make us, or break us,
as He pleases. The vessel cannot say to the potter,
why have you made me so? It must leave it all to the
potter; to be made great, or small, pretty or other-

wise—*the maker knows best.* Even in the same way, the souls abandoned to God are in His hand.

CHAPTER XX.

*Jer. 10:7, 8   O Lord, You have deceived me, and
I was deceived. You are stronger than I, and have
prevailed.   I am become a laughing stock all the
day, everyone mocks me . . . the word of the Lord
is made a reproach to me, and a derision, all the
day.*

It is true, and You, Lord know it, that Your
truths have been made a laughing stock at all times:
they have been the subject of reproach and confusion. Those who have announced them have been
railed at by those who had to hear God's truth. In the
same way, the *souls who live the interior life* are de-
rided by men. This frequently exercises the patience
of those *in* whom God desires to speak, and *through
whom* He speaks: and because they do not see *all* the
success which they *expect* from their words, they re-
gret to have uttered them. But this is a great mistake,
for they ought to be always ready to witness for God,
without expecting any other fruit than being scoffed
at. Still, however holy a man may be, he often repents of his testimony for the Lord, when he sees so
contrary an effect, it is against all his expectation. One

reflects on what one has said, and begins to doubt that it was prompted by God: one thinks to have been mistaken, or at least that God did it to humble one. The *"called of God,"* make a great mistake in measuring the truth of the word spoken by its success: this will only trouble the soul, keep one back, and hinder their testimony for the Truth.

> *Jer. 20:9   And if I say, I will not make mention of Him, nor speak any more in His name, then there is in my heart as it were a burning fire shut up in my bones, and I am weary with forbearing, and I cannot contain.*

I feel assured, that every soul who permits herself to be guided by God without any resistance, and who in her reflections and anxieties has resolved to do, or to leave undone, certain testimonies of God, as it may please him, has experienced that which the prophet here says, and which is expressed so well, that some experienced souls will be delighted to find herein described their own state. As soon as the soul is prevented by shame, fear, confession, etc., to leave undone what God desires of her, there arises in her as it were a burning fire, and she is compelled to do that, which she was not willing to do: and if she resisted any longer, she would feel herself as it were in the regions of hell. The trial is so strong, that the heart cannot bear it: it would break, in continuing the struggle against the power of God. That it is, which comes of resisting God's call in the soul. Whosoever has felt something of this nature in his experience, on whatever subject it may be, must come to the conclu-

sion, that it is in consequence of resisting the work of
God in the soul.

CHAPTER XXX.

Jer. 30:10, 11   *Alas! For that day is great, so that none is like it: it is even the time of Jacob's trouble: but he shall be saved out of it. Therefore fear not, O Jacob, My servant, says the Lord: neither be dismayed, O Israel: for I will save you from afar, and your seed from the land of their captivity: and Jacob shall return, and shall be quiet and at ease, and none shall make him afraid. For I am with you, says the Lord, to save you.*

Every soul abandoned to God has to pass through *tribulation, estrangements*, and *captivity*. But they must give themselves up entirely, and fear not, neither be dismayed: for the Lord will save them from afar, and will enable them to return to Himself, even in His appointed time. And when God makes the soul return from her very death, and from her estrangement and captivity, then shall she be quiet and at ease, and nothing shall dismay her any more: for the Lord Himself is her portion and her rest. All fear has vanished, because the soul experiences afresh the presence of her God, and the deliverance that she finds in Him surpasses all she ever imagined or long for.

CHAPTER XXXI.

Jer. 31: 23, 25   Yet again shall they use this speech in the land of Judah and in the cities thereof, when I shall bring them again out of their captivity: the Lord bless you, O habitation of justice, O mountain of holiness! For I have satiated the weary soul, and every sorrowful soul have I replenished.

When the soul has passed through all those strange wanderings, which were so necessary for her: when her long and weary captivity is ended at last, when she finds herself called and received into God— Oh, then it is when she exclaims: "You are blessed and worthy of praise, oh mountain of holiness! You, oh habitation, in which shines forth the justice of righteousness! There is no righteousness like Yours; every other is hideous and soiled!"

Then, all those sorrowful souls who longed for deliverance in a parched and withered land, where no water flowed, are filled with living streams of holy joy. They have passed through famine and death, hungry and faint—but now find themselves replenished by God. Oh bliss unknown, and inconceivable to those who have not tasted it!

CHAPTER XXXII.

Jer. 32:37-41   I will gather them out of all the countries, where I have driven them. . . I will bring them again to this place, and I will cause them to dwell safely: they shall be My people, and I will be their God. I will give them one heart and one way. . . I will make an everlasting covenant with them, that I will not turn away from them, to do them good. Yes, I will rejoice over them to do them good, and I will plant them in this land assuredly with My whole heart and with My whole soul.

After God has "spit the soul" out of His mouth on account of her fatness and self-righteousness, after she has gone astray among everything on the face of the earth—then God will verily gather her into His bosom, where she shall dwell safely in peace and true faith: in entire assurance, and confidence that nothing whatever shall take her astray again. Of such souls the Lord is truly "their God, and they are His people to delight in doing His will." And He gives them ONE HEART to walk in Him and by Him in newness of life: He leads them in the ONE WAY—the way of perfect unity with God.

And the Lord makes with this soul an everlasting covenant, which is this firm and permanent oneness with Him: God never ceases to work in her, and does her good a thousandfold. Oh, the sure and boundless mercies of God! And You, Lord, are not only doing it. Yes, You rejoice over us to do us good. You are planting and establishing us in Yourself. You are giving all such souls power to do Your holy will. Here is the plenitude of Your Word and of Your Holy Spirit, Your very heart and Your whole soul. Ah, truly! Our trials are past: our bliss runs over.

> *Jer. 32:42   For thus says the Lord: Just as I have brought all this great evil upon this people, so will I bring upon them all the good that I have promised them.*

See how the measure of the evil times, of those crosses borne, of those afflictions and great trials that the Lord permitted and brought this soul through. By all these God has measured and prepared and laid up His bountiful store of mercies: He truly overwhelms her the more with His riches, as those great evils were crushing upon her.

Chapter XXXIII.

*Jer. 33:6   Behold, I will bring it healing and
cure, and I will cure them: and I will reveal to
them abundance of peace and truth.*

God has shown to this soul her wounds, that
she may understand her grievous condition—the bad
that is in her. God is at hand to heal what He has laid
open. From the soul that is somewhat advanced, God
generally hides her faults, that she may lose all recol-
lection of self: then, when it pleases Him, He lets her
see the thousands of wrinkles she did not know. But
God shows them, that He may stroke them away, for
this soul could not bear to see, that anything in her
should displease her Lord: it would draw her attention
away from that chief purpose of losing herself in God.

He also reveals to her, the true prayer of
abounding in peace and in truth, which is consistent
with the manner of approaching His Godhead. The
Lord, is our peace and our truth, and only when all is as
nothing, can the soul approach Him in the peace and
the truth that He gives, and only so long as she abides

in the sense of her own nothingness. Herein is wisdom indeed, when we act in accordance with the revelation of true prayer.

> *Jer. 33:9   And this city shall be to Me for a name of joy, for a praise and for a glory, before all the nations of the earth, which shall hear all the good that I do for them, and shall fear and tremble for all the good and for all the peace that I procure on it.*

God makes known His glory, through all the good which He bestows upon those souls who have abandoned themselves to Him, and all the people who see it and hear of it, and who aspire to the same blessings, shall long for such good things, and for that peace which God has prepared for those who trust solely in Him. But those who have quit the true way of trusting in the things that make for peace with God, who will not again walk in it, and those who have not yet entered on this way, are astonished: they fear and tremble. Oh, what a loss, to have despised or neglected so great Salvation!

CHAPTER XXXIV.

Jer. 34:2   *Behold I will give this city into the hand of the king of Babylon, and he shall burn it with fire.*

Everyone, who attentively reads in the sacred writings of the Prophets will notice, that God does not send forth the most extreme punishments, and the most striking desolations, without promising at the same time deliverance and abundance of blessings: and after God has held out His mercies in vain, the evil overtakes those who are disobedient. This mixture, of cause and effect in all things, may teach man not to trust in the fleeting presence, however sweet, nor to lose hope in tribulation, however severe. Nevertheless, we bring upon ourselves the evil like a flood, and our souls lose all hope for good. But when hope has faded away, when the soul knows her misery and is in the pangs of a wretched contentment, then the promises of the mercies of God are fulfilled. Even so it was, when the soul trusted that the enjoyment of the present, should last forever: then the eventful change came upon her. We have to become indifferent, to the evil things and to the good, whether they be of long duration or otherwise. When that which is evil is done away forever, then that which is good will be all and everlasting.

CHAPTER XXXVI.

*Jer. 36:18   Baruch answered: He pro-
nounced all these words to me with His mouth,
and I wrote them with ink in the book.*

When it is God Himself who works and speaks
through His chosen ones, then it proceeds without
study, and without preparation or arrangement: the
thing then is done without pain, without trouble, and
without hesitation.

*Jer. 36: 21, 23   The king sent Jehudi to
fetch the roll. When Jehudi had read three or four
leaves, then the king cut it with the penknife, and
cast it into the fire.*

The burning of the writings of the servants of
God is no new thing at the present day: and if it could
be done, those who wrote them would be burnt as
well: because they are an offence to those whose way
of living is condemned by the writings, and the lives
of the writers.

*Jer. 36: 27, 28, 32   Then the Word of the Lord
came to Jeremiah, saying: Take another roll, and*

write in it all the former words that were in the first roll, which Jehoiakim the king of Judah has burned. And there were added besides to them many like words.

Oh, Lord God, Your arm has not been shortened! The word of Your doings has to go forth: Your servants will repeat the same, according to Your holy will! Holy Writ has been spread, by the very means that were used to destroy it. And as the church of Christ was established on the blood of her witnesses, so also the Holy Scriptures have become more widely known through the war that has been waged against them.

CHAPTER XXXVII.

Jer. 38:6   *Then they cast Jeremiah into the pit that was in the court of the guard. . . . and in this dungeon there was no water, but mire, and Jeremiah sank in the mire.*

If it is a strange persecution against those who announce the truth, the firmness of these saints is not the least admirable feature in it. They are hunted down and treated shamefully: they are thrown into the pit of mire and confusion, into the deepest nothingness. Yet all these horrors cannot take away their hope, nor their firmness to uphold the Truth. Even such as proceeds from the mouth of God. Yes, they count not their lives too dear, to lay them down in God's holy cause.

Jer. 38: 20, 21, 23   *Jeremiah answered the king: . . . Obey, I beseech you, the voice of the Lord, in that which I speak to you: so it shall be well with you. . . . but if you refuse to go forth you shall be taken by the hand of the king of Babylon.*

After Jeremiah was taken out of the miry pit, the fear of being thrust back again and having to die there did not prevent him from speaking the truth: the love within him has not become callous and quenched: he desires with greater ardor than ever, that the king and the princes who make him suffer so cruelly may obey the voice of the Lord. He beseeches them with words full of kindness. It is not I who speaks to you, it is God, by my mouth: listen to God's voice, so shall it be well with you. But if you refuse, and will not obey, then you will be made captives, and I shall be sorry to see it. For no other cause are the men of God treated with contempt and hatred than for speaking the truth. What they say is to the advantage of those who threat them evilly, despitefully use them: they expose their lives to save these enemies. Yet so great is the blindness of their persecutors, that love and truthfulness are treated as the highest outrage against them.

CHAPTER XXXIX.

Jer. 39:3, 6, 7   *All the princes of the king of Babylon entered into the city . . . Then the king of Babylon slew the sons of Zedekiah in Riblah before his eyes: also the King of Babylon slew all the nobles of Judah. Moreover he put out Zedekiah's eyes.*

The servants of God are not obeyed, but that which was not believed is brought about too soon for those who would not hear. While they say to themselves: "We have peace and plenty," there comes upon them that which they would not believe. They would not have the true peace when it was offered them, when it was in their easy reach.

Jer. 39:12   (Concerning Jeremiah.) Take him, and look well to him, and do him no harm: but do to him even as he shall say to you.

The servants of God find more favor among the barbarians, than with their own allies. God takes such a particular care of them, that they are not destroyed in the ruin which they may have to predict.

Chapter XLII.

Jer. 42: 9, 10, 13, 16   *Thus says the Lord,*
the God of Israel . . . If you will still abide in this
land, then will I build you, and not pull you down,
and I will plant you, and not pull you up: for I
repent of the evil I have done to you. But if you
say, we will not dwell in this land, so that you
obey not the voice of the Lord your God . . . the
sword which you fear shall overtake you.

When the soul remains obedient and willing
to dwell in the land of her nothingness and defeat:
when she seeks no refuge outside of God, but is well
pleased to keep in abandonment to His requirements:
when she has no anxiety nor desire of her own about
what should befall her: Oh, then God will edify her;
He will build up admirably that which appeared so
near a complete destruction: He then plants her and
encloses her within Himself, and makes her take
strong roots: yes, even those souls whom God appeared to have rejected: He is satisfied with—hu-
manly speaking—He repents Himself of the evil that
He permitted to befall them.

But if the soul will not dwell in her allotment and in her abandonment: if she will not obey the voice of the Lord her God, who requires of her still further self-renunciation: if she seeks satisfaction and refuge in such practices as God has desired her to abstain from, or in the creaturely comfort of anything earthly: then, the sword which she feared shall smite her.

Oh, whosoever you are that dwell in sorrow and suffering, abide still further in closer reliance on God—to Him be abandoned forever! If you should accomplish some act by your own strength, which is to take you out of God's keeping: you will only entangle yourself: yes, you will perish by the very things that you did to save yourself. Leave yourself to God and His guidance: that is the cure for your evils—the only means to get rid of them.

CHAPTER XLIII.

*Jer 43:1, 2   When Jeremiah had make an
end of speaking to all the people . . . then spoke
all the proud men, saying to Jeremiah, you speak
falsely: the Lord our God has not sent you to say,
you shall not go into Egypt to sojourn there.*

All those strong in themselves, who are proud
and take hold of their own human wisdom say: "It is
not well to live in this quietude and in this self-renunciation, waiting that God may deliver us: it is an
error, a lie and a falsehood! Let us go down into Egypt,
the land of many devices!" All who say: "We must
leave our simplicity, to return to those schemes and
those methods!" know nothing of God and His Spirit:
they have a spirit that errs, they talk delusion and
death! That was the counsel of old, and the fierce
and the proud talk this way daily.

*Jer. 43:4, 5, 7   All the captains of the forces
. . . obeyed not the voice of the Lord, to dwell in
the land of Judah . . . But they took with them all
the remnant of Judah . . . and they came into the
land of Egypt: for they obeyed not the voice of the
Lord.*

They will not obey the voice within them, the voice of God that exhorts us to dwell in Judah, in perfect abandonment of self. Forward they go in their own strength, taking with them the remnant of Judah, the feeble as well as the strong, who rather believe the voice of the Scribes, that proudly trust in the Law, than the WORD that proceeds as the Truth, and the Way, and the Life, out of the mouth of Jehovah. And they return into Egypt, the land where the multitude dwells. To the winds they cast humility: they will not abandon themselves to the keeping of God their Creator: they hate the simple, the peaceable homes of old Judah. Onward they must go, and down into Egypt, where they are lost in wandering here and there: where their evils can never be cured, growing a thousand times worse than ever before.

SeedSowers

P.O. Box 3317
Jacksonville, FL 32206
800-228-2665
904-598-3456 (fax) www.seedsowers.com

REVOLUTIONARY BOOKS ON CHURCH LIFE

The House Church Movement *(Begier, Richey, Vasiliades, Viola)* 9.95
How to Meet In Homes *(Edwards)* 10.95
An Open Letter to House Church Leaders *(Edwards)* 4.00
When the Church Was Led Only by Laymen *(Edwards)* 4.00
Beyond Radical *(Edwards)* 5.95
Rethinking Elders *(Edwards)* 9.95
Revolution, The Story of the Early Church *(Edwards)* 8.95
The Silas Diary *(Edwards)* 9.99
The Titus Diary *(Edwards)* 8.99
The Timothy Diary *(Edwards)* 9.99
The Priscilla Diary *(Edwards)* 9.99
The Gaius Diary *(Edwards)* 9.99
Overlooked Christianity *(Edwards)* 14.95

AN INTRODUCTION TO THE DEEPER CHRISTIAN LIFE

Living by the Highest Life *(Edwards)* 8.99
The Secret to the Christian Life *(Edwards)* 8.99
The Inward Journey *(Edwards)* 8.99

CLASSICS ON THE DEEPER CHRISTIAN LIFE

Experiencing the Depths of Jesus Christ *(Guyon)* 8.95
Practicing His Presence *(Lawrence/Laubach)* 8.95
The Spiritual Guide *(Molinos)* 8.95
Union With God *(Guyon)* 8.95
The Seeking Heart *(Fenelon)* 9.95
Intimacy with Christ *(Guyon)* 10.95
Spiritual Torrents *(Guyon)* 10.95
The Ultimate Intention *(Fromke)* 11.00

IN A CLASS BY THEMSELVES

The Divine Romance *(Edwards)* 8.95
The Story of My Life as told by Jesus Christ *(Four gospels blended)* 14.95
Acts in First Person *(Book of Acts)* 9.95

COMMENTARIES BY JEANNE GUYON

Genesis Commentary 10.95
Exodus Commentary 10.95
Leviticus - Numbers - Deuteronomy Commentaries 12.95
Judges Commentary 7.95
Job Commentary 10.95
Song of Songs *(Song of Solomon Commentary)* 9.95
Jeremiah Commentary 7.95
James - I John - Revelation Commentaries 12.95

THE CHRONICLES OF THE DOOR *(Edwards)*
The Beginning 8.99
The Escape 8.99
The Birth 8.99
The Triumph 8.99
The Return 8.99

THE WORKS OF T. AUSTIN-SPARKS
The Centrality of Jesus Christ 19.95
The House of God 29.95
Ministry 29.95
Service 19.95
Spiritual Foundations 29.95
The Things of the Spirit... 10.95
Prayer 14.95
The On-High Calling 10.95
Rivers of Living Water 8.95
The Power of His Resurrection 8.95

COMFORT AND HEALING
A Tale of Three Kings *(Edwards)* 8.99
The Prisoner in the Third Cell *(Edwards)* 5.99
Letters to a Devastated Christian *(Edwards)* 5.95
Healing for those who have been Crucified by Christians *(Edwards)* 8.95
Dear Lillian *(Edwards)* 5.95

OTHER BOOKS ON CHURCH LIFE
Climb the Highest Mountain *(Edwards)* 9.95
The Torch of the Testimony *(Kennedy)*............................... 14.95
The Passing of the Torch *(Chen)* 9.95
Going to Church in the First Century *(Banks)* 5.95
When the Church was Young *(Loosley)* 8.95
Church Unity *(Litzman, Nee, Edwards)* 14.95
Let's Return to Christian Unity *(Kurosaki)*........................ 14.95

CHRISTIAN LIVING
The Autobiography of Jeanne Guyon...................................... 14.95
Final Steps in Christian Maturity *(Guyon)* 12.95
Turkeys and Eagles *(Lord)* 8.95
The Life of Jeanne Guyon *(T.C. Upham)* 17.95
Life's Ultimate Privilege *(Fromke)*...................................... 10.00
Unto Full Stature *(Fromke)* 10.00
All and Only *(Kilpatrick)* 7.95
Adoration *(Kilpatrick)* 8.95
Release of the Spirit *(Nee)* 6.00
Bone of His Bone *(Huegel)* modernized................................ 8.95
Christ as All in All *(Haller)* 9.95